How to Care for Your Guinea Pig

CONTENTS

We would like to thank the following for permission to photograph their stock:
Hansards Pet Centre, Romsey

Photographs by:
Peter Gurney
Colin Jeal

©2001 by Kingdom Books PO9 5TT ENGLAND

INTRODUCTION

Guinea pigs, or cavies as they are also known, make excellent pets for young and old alike. They are inexpensive to buy and to keep, need not take up a lot of space, and can be kept either indoors or outdoors. They are good natured and easy to handle. However, before going ahead and buying a guinea pig or two, ask yourself if you really are prepared for the responsibilities that owning a pet entails. The care of a guinea pig is not as complex as, say, the care of a dog or cat, but it will still need feeding and handling and its cage will need to be cleaned out regularly. It will possibly need grooming as well if it is of a long-haired variety.

Do not expect a child to take sole responsibility for the guinea pig's care; children forget easily or get distracted. With a younger child, the ultimate responsibility for any pet must lie with the parents. Also bear in mind that guinea pigs should not be given to children as pets until the children are old enough to handle them safely. A suitable age may be around five years. If younger, the child may accidentally drop the guinea pig, which may injure it seriously or even kill it.

Above: A Sheltie guinea pig. When choosing your pet, bear in mind that long-haired varieties need more care.
Opposite: A Dutch guinea pig.

SELECTION

Having decided that you would be a suitable guinea pig owner you may want to consider what breed or variety you want to purchase. These days, pure-bred guinea pigs come in an abundance of coat varieties and colours, and then there are cross-breeds as well. Your local pet shop probably will not stock more than a couple of pure-breds among the cross-breds but may be able to give you details of local breeders who will be able to supply you with what you want. You can also scan your local paper, as guinea pig breeders often advertise excess stock for sale.

What breed or variety you choose does not really matter, as all will make good pets, cross-bred and pure-bred alike. You should consider, however, that you must be prepared to spend a lot of time grooming your pet if you choose a long-haired breed. For the novice guinea pig owner, a short-haired variety may be preferable.

The different breeds of guinea pigs all have the same basic body shape and size; it is only the coat and colour that vary. Guinea pigs bred for showing should be large and round, with broad, short heads, large eyes, and drooping ears. Pet guinea pigs of the variety that you will usually find in pet shops tend to be slightly smaller, with narrower faces, and ears that are held more or less erect. Unless you plan to take up showing as a hobby the so called 'type' does not matter. The various breeds are as follows:

Smooth Coated: The original short-haired variety comes in almost any imaginable colour variation. Self coloured short-hairs are the same colour all over: Black, Red, Cream, White, Chocolate or some other colour. Among the non-self smooth-coated guinea pigs is the Agouti, whose coat is made up of bi-coloured hairs, giving the 'wild' look of the wild mouse or rabbit. Agouti guinea pigs can be Golden, Silver, Lemon or several other colours.

Himalayan guinea pigs are white with pink eyes, and their feet, ears and faces are black or chocolate, similar to a Siamese cat. Dutch guinea pigs have markings similar to those of the Dutch rabbit and Dutch mouse: white body with coloured sides to the head, the rear half of the body being the same colour as the sides of the head. Tortoiseshell, bi-colour and tricolour guinea pigs have equal squares of two or three colours spread over the body. Brindles are black and red mixed together, giving a mottled appearance. Dalmation guinea pigs are spotted like Dalmatian dogs, and Roans have coloured and white hairs mixed evenly together. Many other colours exist, too.

Two pet Buff guinea pigs.

Satin: A most attractive variety of guinea pig, with a very special, shiny coat that really shimmers. The Satin comes in any colour variety, and indeed any coat type as well, although the traditional Satin is smooth-coated.

Crested: These are smooth-coated with a 'crest' (a circular whirl of fur) in the middle of their foreheads. The English Crested's crest is the same colour as its body while the American Crested has a white crest with a contrasting body.

A Satin Golden Sheltie.
Owners of show quality Shelties have to spend a great deal of time grooming them.

Rex: These have fairly harsh, slightly wavy coats that stand out from the body. They can be of any coat variety or colour. Teddy guinea pigs look almost identical to Rexes but differ genetically. If you mate a Rex to a Teddy, none of the offspring will be wavy-coated; they will all be smooth.

Abyssinian: These are rough-coated, with up to 10 'rosettes' distributed over their bodies. A perfect Abyssinian is not easy to find as each rosette should be in a given position. If you see guinea pigs with less than eight rosettes, placed unevenly across their bodies, they are probably Abyssinian cross-breeds. Abyssinians are normally Selfs, Brindles, Tortoiseshells or Roans, but they can be any colour.

Peruvian: The original long-haired breed. The Peruvian has long fur which covers all of the body, including the head. A Peruvian in full coat looks rather like a mop head and it is difficult to tell one end from the other! The coat can reach a length of 60cm if properly tended. Needless to say, they need a considerable amount of grooming, and breeders of Peruvians and other long-haired breeds keep the long fur wound onto spools to stop it getting dirty and tangled. The coat of the pet Peruvian will probably never grow so long but it will still need daily grooming. Peruvians can be any colour but specific patterns such as Dutch are seldom, if ever, seen as these animals are bred for coat not colour.

This show quality White Crested guinea pig just knows it's an aristocrat!

Sheltie: Another long-haired variety. The Sheltie's long hair does not cover its face: the fur grows in the same direction as the smooth-coated guinea pig's, but it is the same length as the Peruvian's.

Coronets: Shelties with a crest on their head, like the smooth-coated crested guinea pig. Unlike their short-coated counterparts, Coronets are not classified as English or American, as no consideration is given to colour when breeding any of the long-haired breeds.

Texels and Alpacas: Shelties and Peruvians originally were bred to Rexes to produce Texels (curly-coated Shelties) and Alpacas (curly-coated Peruvians).

Male Or Female

Whether you choose a male guinea pig (boar) or female (sow) is of little importance, as both sexes make equally good pets. To tell whether your guinea pig is male or female, gently turn it over onto its back. In the young boar, the genitalia are in the shape of a circle. In the sow, the genitalia are Y-shaped. In the adult guinea pig, sexing is easier. The boar's testicles will show as two large balls, one each side of his genitalia, and his penis will show if you press gently in the middle. The sow, naturally, will lack testicles, and when viewed from above will have a slightly different body shape from the boar. If you are ever unsure of the sex of a guinea pig, try to compare two or three, as sexing will be much easier when you have both sexes to compare. Both females and males have two nipples on their lower abdomen, so the presence of these is no indication of gender.

One Or Two

Guinea pigs love company so, unless you are going to spend a lot of time handling your animal you should really decide to get two. Choosing two females is usually your best option here. Two males may get on well all their life if kept together from an early age, but some male guinea pigs will not accept the presence of another male once adult. Keeping one of each sex will mean a never-ending supply of little guinea pig babies. Contrary to popular belief, it is possible to keep a male and a female together on a permanent basis, but it will need careful planning. The male and the female must not be introduced at too early an age, as the male will mate her at the earliest possible opportunity, and a pregnancy at a very early age may mean the death of the female, her litter, or both.

Once one litter has been born, the male will immediately mate with the female again, so a new litter will soon be on its way. Unless the female takes a natural break now and then, which some do, you will have to separate the pair occasionally to give the female a rest from breeding, or she may die from exhaustion. Also, do you know what to do with all the resulting baby guinea

Left: Madame Bom-bom, a cross-bred Abyssinian, knows she's beautiful.

Opposite: A pet Golden long-haired guinea pig.

Below: A Rex guinea pig. Note the harsh, slightly wavy texture of his coat.

pigs? Unless you have enough friends who are willing to give homes to them, or know of a pet shop that will take them, you could soon be overrun with guinea pigs! It is possible to ask a vet to neuter your male guinea pig, an option that may be worth considering.

If you find that you are unable to keep two guinea pigs together, for whatever reason, you can consider keeping a rabbit and a guinea pig. It is often said that rabbits will harm guinea pigs, intentionally or unintentionally. However, if you choose a small breed of rabbit, introduce the rabbit and the guinea pig to each other as youngsters, and provide some sort of a house or nest small enough for the guinea pig, but not the rabbit, to get into, they will usually become the best of friends with no problems.

What To Look For

The guinea pig that you are buying will usually be six to ten weeks old. Never accept an animal younger than this, as it really should not have been separated from its mother at such an early age. If you are selecting an older animal, make sure that males and females have been kept in single sex groups, to avoid the surprise of finding that you have bought not just one guinea pig but a whole family!

Carefully examine the animal that you wish to buy. The eyes should be bright and clear, with no discharge. The nose should be dry and clean. The ears should be clean. All guinea pigs have a small hairless area just behind their ears, so this is nothing to worry about, but reject any animal that has hairless patches anywhere else on the body as this may indicate any one of several serious skin problems. The fur should be clean, and so should the guinea pig's rear end. Any dirt around the anus may indicate diarrhoea. If you are unsure of the guinea pig's age, check the claws. A young animal will have short, sharp, straight claws. Older animals will have thicker, blunt claws which often start to curl.

The guinea pig that you choose may well be very nervous. Do not worry unduly about this as most small animals are very nervous to start with. Once your new pet has become accustomed to you it will calm down.

Opposite: Free Range Fred, a Coronet guinea pig, explores his surroundings.

EQUIPMENT

Guinea pigs in Britain are usually kept in hutches in the garden, in a garden shed, or in the garage. It is perfectly all right to keep your guinea pig in the garden if its hutch is made to withstand all kinds of weather, or in a garden shed, but do not keep guinea pigs in a garage if a car is kept there, as the petrol fumes will be harmful to the animal. But why keep your guinea pig outside?

Provided their cages are cleaned regularly, guinea pigs have very little smell, and there is no reason at all why they should not be kept indoors. Guinea pigs that are kept indoors will make better pets, as they will see more of their owner and get more used to people. The kitchen is usually the best room in which to keep your guinea pig cage, as the surfaces are easy to wipe clean, and the guinea pig certainly likes living near to the fridge! He will soon learn to recognise the sound of the fridge door opening, and will start to squeak, begging for vegetables or fruit!

The Hutch

If your guinea pig is to be kept outdoors, you will need a good quality hutch. These are available in many sizes from pet shops. The hutch (or cage) for one to two guinea pigs should be as big as possible, and not less than 60cm x 60cm. The hutch will need to be raised from the ground on legs or placed on top of something, such as an old tea-chest or table. The roof should be covered in roofing felt to protect it from rain and damp, and should be either sloping or pitched to prevent water from gathering on top. The wood should preferably be 1.5cm to 2.5cm thick and it should have been treated with non-poisonous wood preserver. The front of the hutch should be partly of strong wire-netting (not flimsy chicken wire) to stop cats or dogs from reaching in, and partly solid wood, to give the guinea pig shelter from rain and snow. Some hutches come with a separate 'bedroom' sectioned off from the rest of the hutch by a dividing wall with an opening in it. For further protection the hutch should be placed with its back against a building. It should be constructed so that it is easy to open and to keep clean.

If the hutch is to be kept inside a shed or similar outbuilding, it can be a simpler construction in plywood with a flat roof and wire-netting right across the front. It is still best to treat the wood with wood preserver, however, as this will greatly prolong the life of the hutch.

The Indoor Cage

It is possible to buy indoor cages for guinea pigs, though these are not as common as hutches. The ideal indoor cage will have the same measurements as the hutch but will have a plastic tray with a wire canopy. If you fail to find a suitable indoor cage, you can either use a hutch or make your own cage. All that you need is a simple box made of wood that has been treated with wood preserver, with part of the front covered in wire so that you can see your pets. Just make sure that the cage is at least 40cm tall to prevent your guinea pig from jumping out!

Furnishing The Hutch Or Cage

A guinea pig cage will not need much furniture. The most important item is some sort of suitable floor covering. This can be woodshavings, or newspaper covered in straw. Do not use sawdust: the grains are too fine and will find their way inside the guinea pig's eyes and nostrils. If using newspaper, make sure that it is well covered with straw, or your animal will chew the paper. For this reason, it is not a good idea to cover the newspaper with hay as that will soon be eaten. Hay should always be provided in the guinea pig's cage, but this can be placed either on top of the wood shavings or straw or in a special hay-rack fastened to the wall of the hutch or cage. You can make a hay-rack in the simple form of a square basket, using wire-netting. A house or nest box within the cage is not strictly necessary but many guinea pigs enjoy having one. You can make one out of wood. Never give them plastic boxes as these will be too warm, and avoid cardboard as this will be chewed.

A Sheltie shows off her lovely coat. Shelties have been described as 'Peruvians with back-swept hairstyles' and, as with Peruvians, their hair can grow up to 60cm long.

The food bowl can be a metal hopper hung onto the door or side of the cage or a heavy earthenware bowl that cannot be knocked over. Plastic bowls will certainly be chewed and free-standing metal bowls will be knocked over.

Water should be provided in a gravity water bottle, available from your pet shop. Never provide water in a bowl as this will be soiled in no time and, if it is knocked over, your guinea pig will be left in a soggy cage with no water. The water in the bottle should be changed daily and the bottle cleaned by means of a bottle brush or old, discarded toothbrush. You will need to clean out your guinea pig's cage as soon as it starts to look and smell dirty. How often will depend on the size of the cage or hutch and the number of animals kept in it. For an average sized cage housing one or two animals a twice-weekly clean will be the minimum. Every other month or so the cage or hutch should be thoroughly cleaned and disinfected, using a disinfectant that is harmless to animals. This should also always be done if the original occupant of the cage has died and you wish to house a new animal in it.

The slightly wavy texture of the coat shows us that this is a Rex guinea pig.

Guinea pigs are vegetarian, which means that they eat no meat or fish. Their diet should consist mainly of hay, grain and vegetables. Guinea pigs, along with monkeys, apes and human beings, are unusual in that their bodies cannot produce Vitamin C. Because of this, all guinea pigs need to receive a diet rich in Vitamin C, or serious health problems will follow. The easiest way to achieve this is to feed your guinea pig plenty of fruit and vegetables.

Hay is essential for guinea pigs. It provides roughage, aids digestion, and also gives the guinea pig something to nibble on. Guinea pigs like to eat more or less constantly. The hay should be of good quality, neither dusty nor mouldy. Check that it smells fresh. Hay should be available in an unlimited supply.

An American Crested guinea pig with her litter.
Note that the pups have not taken after her but tend towards the Agouti colouring natural to wild cavies. This sometimes happens with 'mixtures'.

A good quality guinea pig mix should always be available too. Such a mix usually contains grains and flakes, as well as pellets. Some people prefer to feed their guinea pigs on pelleted food only. Special guinea pig mixes, some of them with added Vitamin C, are available in pet shops. Do not give your guinea pig a hamster mix, as this will contain peanuts and sunflower seeds. Peanuts are too fattening for guinea pigs and sunflower seeds can be harmful if given in large quantities. Both can also get stuck to the guinea pig's teeth.

A Silver Agouti guinea pig. Wild cavies are Agouti, which means that their coats are made up of bi-coloured hairs - in the case of Silvers, black shafts with light grey tips.

Suitable fruit and vegetables include carrots, cabbage, swede, celery, cucumber, tomato, apple, pear and lettuce. Other guinea pig favourites include fresh grass (hand picked, not cut with a lawn mower, as this could contaminate the grass) and dandelion leaves. If you pick grass and dandelion leaves for your guinea pigs, do not go close to roads, as the greens there will be contaminated by traffic fumes, and avoid areas where dogs are exercised. Always wash hand-picked greens as a health precaution before giving them to your guinea pig.

It is best to obtain your cavy from a breeder. The above photograph shows how breeders typically house their guinea pigs.

Guinea pigs can be fed once or twice daily. If they are fed twice, give fresh vegetables (such as half an average-sized carrot per guinea pig) at one meal, and top up the bowl of guinea pig mixture at the other meal. Guinea pigs are very greedy little animals and will quickly become fat if overfed. A salt licking stone can be hung in the hutch or cage, as most guinea pigs will enjoy licking these. Salt forms an essential part of the guinea pig's metabolism.

Cavies enjoy dandelions (right) and clover (far right). Never collect wild plants for your guinea pigs from an area that may have been sprayed with pesticides.

A glamourous Coronet guinea pig.

GENERAL CARE

Assuming your guinea pig is healthy and kept in a clean cage, little special care will be needed. The long-haired guinea pig will need daily grooming, and a metal comb and soft brush are best for this. The short-haired varieties will benefit from brushing when they are moulting, and also perhaps once a week or so, to remove any loose dead hairs. Some guinea pigs will get dirty enough to need bathing, especially if they are long-haired. A guinea pig should not be bathed too often, and certainly not more than once a month, or the natural oils found in the coat may be removed, causing skin problems. You must also take care that it does not get cold.

To bath your guinea pig, place it in a plastic washing-up bowl or sink filled with enough luke-warm water to reach its chest. Using your hand or a jug, gently wet the body all over, taking care to avoid the eyes and ears. When the coat is thoroughly soaked, massage in a small amount of shampoo. Use either a baby shampoo or a mild shampoo formulated for small pets or cats. Avoid using dog shampoos as these may be too strong and therefore poisonous to the guinea pig, and never use shampoos intended for adult humans. When you have finished shampooing your guinea pig, carefully rinse all traces of shampoo from its coat. Then remove your pet from the bowl and squeeze out any excess water from the coat with your hands. Wrap your guinea pig in a towel and rub it dry. If it is a warm day, your guinea pig can be allowed to dry off inside its clean cage. If not, you must dry it with a hairdryer to make sure that it does not catch a cold. When using the hairdryer, take care not to burn your pet, and always keep the guinea pig on your lap.

A Lilac Self guinea pig.

Your guinea pig will appreciate a change of scenery from time to time.

Cross-bred Abyssinians like Dandy, pictured above, are sometimes referred to as 'ridgebacks'. He has insufficient rosettes for a pure-bred and those that he has form a ridge along his back.

Your guinea pig's claws will need regular trimming, usually around once a month when adult. (An adult guinea pig is one which is more than eight months old.) If left to grow too long, the guinea pig's claws will start to curl, and may twist awkwardly, making it difficult to walk. Trim the claws using nail-clippers intended for humans or nail-trimmers intended specially for cats and smaller animals, which are available from pet shops. In light-coloured animals, you can clearly see the blood-filled quick inside the claw. Cut the claw a couple of millimetres from the end of the quick. If the guinea pig has black claws, you will have to guess where to cut as it will be impossible to see the quick. If you are unsure, ask an experienced guinea pig breeder or vet to advise you how to do it. If you should happen to cut too much, the claw will start to bleed. This bleeding will need to be stopped, which is best achieved by using a styptic pencil.

Handling Your Guinea Pig

If your guinea pig is a small baby, you can pick it up by closing your hand over its body. Once it is adult, you will need to slide one hand underneath, just behind the front legs, and lift it with your other hand supporting its bottom. You can then either keep your pet close to your body, which is the safest option for a guinea pig that is nervous, or place it on your lap if it is already tame. Your guinea pig will soon become tame if handled frequently, and if you feed it titbits by hand.

Exercise

Guinea pigs love to exercise now and then. If you have a room in the house where no electrical cables are accessible and there are no places to hide (such as under furniture) you can let your guinea pig run around that room every now and then. If not, you can buy or make a guinea pig run to place in your garden when the weather is nice. Such a run should be constructed of wire-netting, with a covered top to stop predators such as cats from harming your pet. Do make sure that the grass is dry before placing the guinea pig in his run - guinea pigs can die from chills or colds caught in this way. If your guinea pig is outside in a run on a sunny day, make sure that it has access to shade and water. If your guinea pig is normally kept indoors, do not put it outside unless the temperature is at least 15°C, or it may catch a cold.

HEALTH

A lovely Tricolour Abyssinian.

Properly fed and cared for, your guinea pig should stay healthy throughout the five years or so of his life. However, like all animals, guinea pigs sometimes become ill. I have listed some of the most common problems below but, if you are ever unsure about the health of your pet, see a vet as soon as possible.

Diarrhoea: Usually caused by too much green stuff. If your guinea pig is not used to greens, take care when introducing them, especially fresh grass. Give only a small amount at a time until its stomach has got used to it. If your guinea pig develops diarrhoea, give no greens at all until this has settled, but feed plenty of hay, dry food and water. If it persists, consult your vet.

Constipation: The opposite of diarrhoea, usually caused by lack of greens, but it can also be caused by lack of exercise. If you see no droppings in the guinea pig's cage, or only a few small, very hard ones (a guinea pig's droppings are normally dark brown in colour, elongated in shape, and moist but firm) then you may suspect constipation. The guinea pig may also sit still with its back hunched up. For quick relief, give a few drops of medicinal liquid paraffin. In less severe cases, a good feed of wet vegetables such as lettuce and cucumber should do the trick. Do not be alarmed if you see your guinea pig eating its own droppings. This is a practice known as coprophagy, whereby the animal extracts further nutrients from its partially-digested droppings.

Worms: Guinea pigs sometimes suffer from worms, especially if allowed outside in a run on a lawn where the grass may have been contaminated by cats or other animals. The small, white worms can be seen in the guinea pig's droppings. See a vet, who will prescribe a suitable liquid wormer, usually one intended for kittens. Do not attempt to worm it yourself without proper advice.

Lice: A common problem in guinea pigs. Lice are a couple of millimetres long and white in colour, and they can be seen moving around in the guinea pig's fur. Unlike fleas, which guinea pigs seldom catch, lice do not jump. You can spray your guinea pig with a suitable flea spray, or bath it in an insecticidal shampoo for cats or small animals. Any treatment will need to be done twice within 14 days. Ask your vet or pet shop assistant for advice.

There are other types of parasites that your guinea pig may catch (sometimes from its bedding, sometimes from other animals) such as so-called static lice, which are small, brown and firmly attached to your guinea pig's hair. These can be more difficult to remove, and may require more frequent baths. The very best way to treat this problem is to dose your guinea pig with Ivermectin, a medication that will kill off any parasites. This drug can only be obtained from vets or from The Cambridge Cavy Trust (address at the back of

this book), the special guinea pig hospital, and can be given either orally or as an injection.

Other skin problems: Fur loss, reddening of the skin, and itchiness may indicate one of several problems such as mange and fungal infection. See a vet, who will attempt to find the cause of the problem and prescribe suitable treatment.

Eye infections: Sore, runny eyes may occur because the guinea pig has been kept in a draught (close to a window, for example) or because he has damaged his eyes on straw or there is something in them, or it could be a symptom of another disease. See a vet, who will investigate further.

Overgrown or broken teeth: A guinea pig has 20 teeth; four in front (two in the upper jaw and two in the lower) and 16 at the back of its mouth (four on each side in both the upper and lower jaw.) If it is not given enough hard food (such as carrots) its

A young Crested guinea pig.

teeth may grow too long. If the front teeth grow too long, this will be obvious when looking at them. They can be cut down to size easily using wire cutters. It can be difficult to tell when the back teeth arc overgrown, Signs may include the guinea pig chewing its food into small pieces then spitting it out, or trying to eat but not managing to do so. In any case, over-long teeth will cause it feeding problems, so the teeth must trimmed. See a vet if you are at all unsure.

A guinea pig may also occasionally break off one of his long front teeth. The others may then have to be trimmed down to prevent them from growing too long, as they will not be worn down naturally if one tooth is missing. If the guinea pig finds it hard to eat, give it a mash made of bran, finely chopped vegetables and water.

Guinea pig lameness: May be caused by a lack of vitamin C in the guinea pig's diet. The guinea pig's hind legs will go lame, the fur will be dry and the skin scaly. See a vet for vitamin C injections, which hopefully (though not invariably) will rectify the problem.

Mouth fungus: Can be seen as brown matter covering the guinea pig's lips, making them sore and causing the animal difficulty in eating. See a vet who will prescribe a suitable cream with which to treat this condition.

Alternative Medicine

There is a growing interest these days in alternatives to traditional medicine for animals as well as for humans. Sometimes alternative medicine, or a mixture of traditional and alternative, can be very effective. Peter Gurney, one of Great Britain's best known experts on guinea pigs, has written a book called *Piggy Potions* which deals specifically with herbal and natural therapies for guinea pigs.

The Rex guinea pig pictured left has enlarged lower eyelids, a condition known as 'fatty eye'. This does not bother the guinea pig at all but would disqualify any cavy from the show ring.

BREEDING

Although not a pure-bred cavy, this guinea pig is a very handsome pet.

Before deciding to breed from your guinea pigs, consider carefully whether you can find homes for the resulting offspring. Your local pet shop, for example, may take them, but check this out in advance! You will not get rich by breeding guinea pigs as the babies sell for very small sums of money, even if pure-bred.

Selecting Your Breeding Animals

The guinea pigs that you decide to breed from should be healthy and have good temperaments. They should not be too small in size (especially the sow, as this can cause her problems when giving birth) and they must be of the correct age. A boar can be used for breeding from around three months or whenever he starts to take an interest in the opposite sex! The sow should be at least four months old, but not more than eight to ten months, when mated for the first time. Her pelvic bones will fuse in position at the age of twelve months, which means that she may never be able to give birth for the first time after this age, even though she can become pregnant. Once she has had one litter you can continue to breed from her as long as she is in good condition, or up to around the age of three years. Do not let her have more than four litters a year at the most.

Mating

The sow will come into heat (oestrus) every 14-16 days, so the best way to ensure that she mates is to leave her together with the boar for at least three weeks. To be really safe, leave her with him until it is obvious that she is pregnant.

You will not know whether your sow has become pregnant for several weeks. The guinea pig's usual gestation period is 63 to 72 days, although this can vary and it may be as long as 76 days. As a general rule, the smaller the litter, the longer the gestation. You may be able to tell that the sow has started to put on weight after 40 days of pregnancy. At 50 days, you should be able to feel the babies move inside her if you place your hands against her abdomen.

A White Self guinea pig.

Preparing For The Birth

As you probably will not know when the mating took place, it can be difficult to predict the birth. The best way to get some sort of an idea is to check the positioning of the sow's pelvic bones. These are situated right at the end of her body, just where a tail would have been if guinea pigs had one. The two soft bones are normally positioned very close together, and you will not be able to insert a finger in between them. However, when the sow is nearly ready to give birth (up to four days in advance) the pelvic bones will start to separate, until the distance in between them is so great that you can insert two fingers.

The sow will make no nest in her cage, so you will only need to make sure that the cage is as clean as possible, with plenty of soft hay, food and water available. Water is especially important: giving birth is thirsty work!

A show standard Cream Self guinea pig.

The Birth

Most guinea pig litters are born during the night, and often the first thing you know of the litter is that when you say 'hello' to your guinea pig first thing in the morning she has a complete family with her. There will be little or no trace of the birth as there is very little bleeding and the sow will eat the placentas. Each baby is born enclosed in a birth sac, and the sow will rip this open and vigorously lick the baby to make it breathe. She may also nip the baby with her teeth, or even kick it with her feet, if it fails to respond quickly enough. Most sows make excellent mothers.

New-born guinea pigs are fully developed, covered in fur and with open eyes. They will suckle for four to five weeks but will start to nibble on their parents' food as early as a few hours after the birth. They look like miniature copies of their parents. The average litter consists of two or three babies but it can be anything from one to seven. As their development is so advanced, they need no special diet but will share their mother's food. They should be allowed to remain with her until six weeks of age, when they will be fully weaned and ready to go to new homes.

Useful Addresses

Should you wish for more information about the care of guinea pigs, you can contact The Cambridge Cavy Trust, at the address below. The British Association of Rodentologists is also housed at this address. The prime object of this organisation is to expand the knowledge about the general and veterinary care of rodents through teaching courses which are available to the general public.

The Cambridge Cavy Trust (British Association of Rodentologists)
Top Farm Bungalow
Top Farm Lane
Off Ermine Street
Alconbury
Huntingdon
Cambridgeshire
PEl7 5EW
ENGLAND
Telephone: 01480 455346

BIBLIOGRAPHY

GUINEA PIGS
Kay Ragland
KW-016 ISBN 0-86622-830-6
This highly colourful book is easy to read and loaded with practical, easy-to-apply information and sensible advice. It is aimed at the beginner and covers every topic of interest, including pure-bred cavies, grooming the cavy, and hints on the care of orphan cavies.
Hardcover: 140mm x 210mm;
128 pages

THE PROPER CARE OF GUINEA PIGS
Peter Gurney
TW-108S ISBN 0-79383-151-2
This book, illustrated with colour photos, most of them taken by the author, is a practical, down-to-earth guide to everything you need to know about looking after guinea pigs. It is written with love and seasoned with humour.
Softcover: 130mm x 180mm;
256 pages

GUINEA PIGS GETTING STARTED
Anmarie Barrie
TT-008 ISBN 0-86622-420-3
This colourful, informative book, aimed at the beginner, is designed to start you off in the all-absorbing hobby of keeping guinea pigs.
Softcover: 170mm x 250mm,
98 pages

THE SEX LIFE OF GUINEA PIGS
Peter Gurney
GB-090 ISBN: 1-85279-133-0
This book is a fascinating guide to the courtship, mating, pregnancy, birth and rearing of this popular pet.
Hardcover: 150mm x 230mm,
48 pages

also,
PIGGY POTIONS: Natural Remedies for Guinea Pigs
Peter Gurney
GB-001 ISBN 1-85279-004-0
In this cleverly illustrated book Peter Gurney gives expert advice on herbal and natural remedies, including how best to administer them.
Hardcover: 150mm x 230mm;
48 pages

A STEP BY STEP GUIDE TO GUINEA PIGS
Anmarie Barrie
SK-013 ISBN 0-86622-450-5
Author Anmarie Barrie provides a solid base of practical, easy-to-apply advice that takes readers step by step through the selection, housing, feeding, breeding and health care of pet guinea pigs. This book shows many colour and coat varieties in a full-colour layout.
Softcover: 140mm x 210mm;
64 pages

THE REALLY USEFUL GUINEA PIG GUIDE
Myra Mahoney
GB084 ISBN: 1-85279-127-6
In this cleverly illustrated book Myra Mahoney, who has bred and shown guinea pigs for over 30 years, offers expert advice on all aspects of looking after cavies. This best selling title is a must for the reference library of both novice and experienced guinea pig enthusiasts.
Hardcover: 175mm x 260mm
48 pages